Perspectives

Water

The Key to Life?

Series Consultant: Linda Hoyt

Flying Start
to Literacy®

Contents

Introduction

Water: the key to life?

Water is everywhere. It is inside us, and it is inside plants and animals. It is in the ground and in the air. It is so important to life on Earth, we call it the key to life.

But in some places, many people cannot get clean water to drink.

Is water the most important thing in the world? What should we do to save it?

Freshwater facts

Written by Kerrie Shanahan

All living things need water to survive, and without it, there would be no life.

Which of these freshwater facts do you find the most interesting?

- Water makes up 60% of your body.
- Your brain and heart are made up of over 70% water.
- Your bones have over 30% water.

- Less than 3% of all water on Earth is fresh water.
- 99% of all fresh water is found frozen in ice, or underground.

The longest freshwater river is the Nile River. It's over 6,000 kilometres long.

About 70% of all the water we use is for agriculture.

Did you know?

About 800 million people don't have access to safe water.

The world's deepest freshwater lake is Lake Baikal in Russia. It holds 20% of all the fresh water on Earth.

The three main types of freshwater habitats are lakes and ponds, rivers and streams, and wetlands.

Water-saving choice:

Jade and her family live in Melbourne, Australia, where it is hot and dry in summer and sometimes freshwater supplies get very low. They think clean water is precious and save every drop they can.

How can you and your family save fresh water?

There is a drought in my city, so we are careful about how we use water. When we have a shower, we set a timer so that we know when to turn off the taps. And when my little brother has a bath, we only half fill it.

My job is to water the plants in our garden. I do this in the morning. If I did this when it was really hot, the water would dry up quickly and wouldn't soak into the soil. It would be wasted.

If we have a leaky tap, Grandpa fixes it right away. Did you know that a dripping tap can waste about four litres of water a day?

Our family makes good water-saving choices because we know that every little bit helps.

Speak out!

Read what these students have to say about why we need clean water.

How can water kill you? Well, the answer is that some water isn't clean. It can have poisonous things or bacteria in it. A human needs water to survive. But not just any water – fresh and clean water. If you drink dirty water, you could get very sick.

Water is not just for drinking. Plants, trees and flowers all need water just like we do. All living things need water.

All the food we eat needs water. Plants and vegetables need it to grow. They would die without it. If we don't have water, we don't have food.

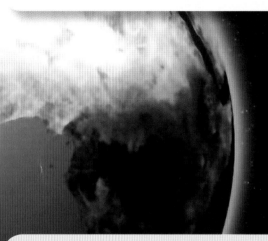

Let's talk about Earth. Seventy per cent of it is water. Water is the starting point, the key to life. That is the reason why scientists at NASA who study space look for signs of water on other planets. They are looking for life, too.

Clean water saves lives!

Written by Nick D'Alto

Some people live in places where there is very little fresh water. And some people live where the water they do have is dirty. This water can make them sick, or even die.

Here are three simple but clever solutions.

Using sunshine to clean water

Did you know that the sun can clean water? If you leave a bottle of dirty water in direct sunlight for six hours, the sun's ultraviolet (UV) rays can kill most of the germs. This is called solar water disinfection, or SoDis. This simple way of cleaning dirty water works well, but only if the correct type of plastic bottle is used.

Straw filters

Can you imagine using a straw that turns dirty water into clean water? Well, scientists have invented a straw that has a filter. When you suck water up through the straw, the germs in the water stay trapped inside the straw and they do not reach your mouth. So the water you drink is clean and you won't get sick. This simple idea is saving lives around the world.

Turning air into water

Have you ever seen drops of water on the grass on a cold morning when it has not rained? Where does this water come from? The answer is the air. When water vapour in the air cools at night, drops of water form.

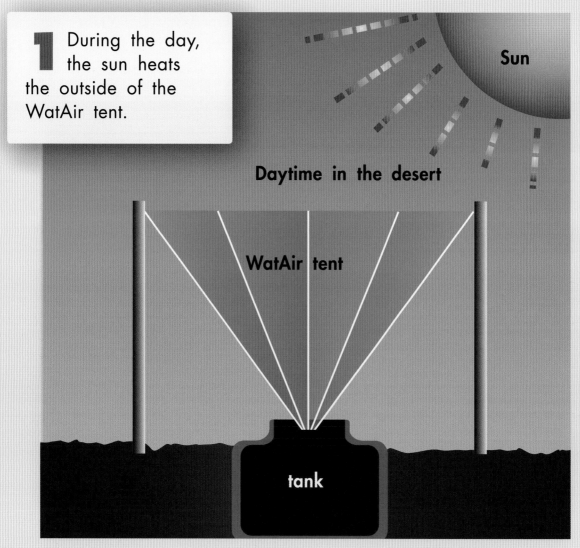

1 During the day, the sun heats the outside of the WatAir tent.

Sun

Daytime in the desert

WatAir tent

tank

This process led to the invention of an upside-down tent called WatAir.

This tent is easy to set up and it can be taken anywhere it is needed. It can collect 45 litres of water each night; that's about 180 glasses of water (250mL glasses).

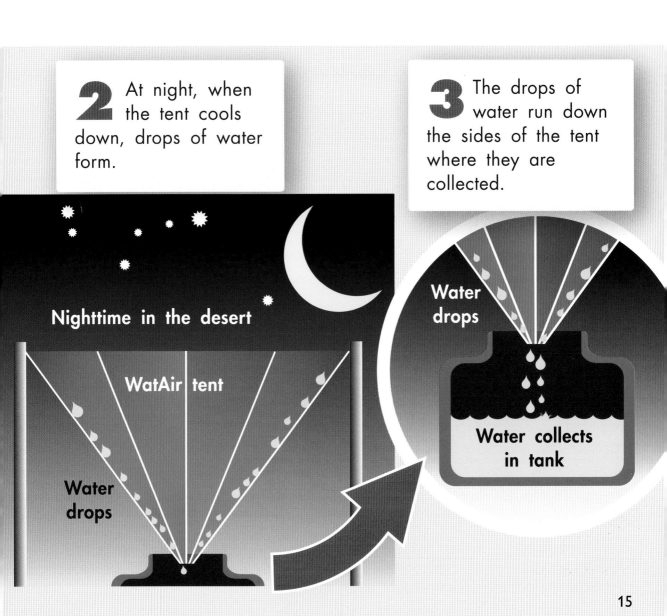

2 At night, when the tent cools down, drops of water form.

3 The drops of water run down the sides of the tent where they are collected.

Nighttime in the desert

WatAir tent

Water drops

Water drops

Water collects in tank

How to write about your opinion

State your opinion

Think about the main question in the introduction on page 4 of this book. What is your opinion?

Research

Look for other information that you need to back up your opinion.

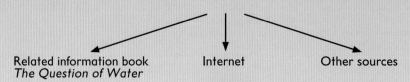

| Related information book *The Question of Water* | Internet | Other sources |

Make a plan

Introduction

How will you "hook" the reader to get them interested?

Write a sentence that makes your opinion clear.

List reasons to support your opinion.

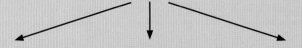

| Support your reason with examples. | Support your reason with examples. | Support your reason with examples. |

Conclusion

Write a sentence that makes your opinion clear. Leave your reader with a strong message.

Publish

Publish your writing.

Include some graphics or visual images.